Candida Detox

A Doctor's Guide to Cleansing Candida and Restoring Your Health

Diana Stafford, MD, and Andrew Stafford

Legal Disclaimer

Medical Disclaimer

This eBook is for educational purposes only and not intended as personal medical advice. The information discussed is not intended to replace the advice of your healthcare provider. Individual responses to supplements and dietary and lifestyle interventions vary. The information discussed is by no means exhaustive. Testing and interventions are some of the most common and are meant to be evaluated in the context of your individual situation.

Table of Contents

Introduction: Why Candida?

Candida albicans, the yeast that causes candidiasis, otherwise known as a yeast infection, has in the modern era become a silent harbinger of illness. This simple yeast relates to numerous health conditions and diseases, some directly caused by Candida and some secondary conditions to which candidiasis contributes. Candida-related health issues have been sending people to healthcare professionals for many decades. The goal of this book is to educate patients and providers about the scope of the prevalence of Candida in humans, the mechanisms that contribute to symptoms and disease, and provide a detailed treatment route for providers to treat their patients.

If you or someone you know has symptoms related to Candida, *Candida Detox* unpacks the science you need to know to figure out how this happened and provides guidance on how to detox the Candida and restore health.

Who is this book for?

People with known or suspected candidiasis, yeast infection, a white tongue, UTI, or another related health issue.

People who have a weak immune system and want a boost

Practitioners and coaches who want condensed, actionable guidance on treating Candida

Doctors who prescribe antibiotics and want to understand the long-term effects of their use

You should also read this book if –

You have frequent digestive problems

You have known or suspected food allergies

You have frequent skin issues including dry skin, eczema, and rashes

You have frequent headaches, muscle or joint pains

You are frequently tired, unfocused, foggy, low energy, teary, poor memory, anxious, or have other mood issues

Chapter 1: Scientific Foundations

We all want to be healthy and ensure the Candida in our body is balanced and not overgrown. To help us accomplish that goal, it is important to first understand some of the basics around Candida, how it presents, the normal and abnormal functions of our body, types of medicine and diagnostic tools used to detect it, and several other topics. Some of this information you've probably not been exposed to, even if you are a practitioner. So, buckle up, friend, as we dive deep into science in this chapter!

What is Candida?

Candida, Candida albicans, yeast (it's only a single species of yeast, there are many more), or fungus (yeast is a single-celled fungus), are all terms you might hear that describe Candida, and Candida is everywhere. It's in every animal that's been tested, mostly in the gut, but also in other tissues. It's in the soil, in the air, in the water, including seawater, and in many other plants, both living and decomposing.

The thing about Candida, though, is that it is usually considered commensal or symbiotic in that it helps protect the organisms it lives with. In humans, Candida lives in the mucosa like the mouth, sinuses, and gut, which means Candida is busy fighting off pathogens, whether that is other fungi, bacteria, or viruses, that would be trying to infect the mucosa. In some people, this symbiosis is disrupted, and the Candida can get out of control causing issues, or their body can flag the Candida as harmful and start attacking it, also causing issues. We'll spend the rest of the book diving deeper into why this happens and how we can overcome it.

Why is Candida Harmful?

In many healthy people, with good diets, and healthy lifestyles, Candida is generally not, or it's only mildly harmful, but in people with overgrowth or those who have lost the commensal relationship, it can cause issues. Part of these issues stem from the production of microscopic toxins called mycotoxins by many species of Candida. These mycotoxins, like aflatoxin and gliotoxin, disrupt the healthy function of your body and cause symptoms or even disease. Candida also creates an alcohol called acetaldehyde that is even more neurotoxic than the alcohol you drink. With a normal, healthy candida population, the amount of acetaldehyde is very minute and processed easily by your liver and kidneys, but in someone with overgrowth, the amount can be 10 or 100 times more, leading to illness and disease. There's a condition called Auto-Brewery Syndrome where Candida, or a few other bacteria or fungi, ferment carbohydrates into actual ethanol, the same as you'd drink, and these people end up intoxicated 24x7 accruing damage to their liver and other organs. For these reasons, Candida should be among the list of suspects for practitioners, if a patient presents with a long-standing history of illness symptoms like those we are about to cover.

What Symptoms can Candida Cause or Worsen?

This list is by no means exhaustive, but it will be tied to the Candida questionnaire in the next chapter.

- Changes to smell, taste, sight, or hearing
- Blurry vision, floaters, or flashing lights off to the side of the visual field
- Brain fog
- Feeling unwell, malaise, soreness
- Mood issues
- Anxiety or panic attacks
- Depression
- Anger or rage
- Poor concentration
- Headaches or migraines
- Confusion
- Itching of the eyes, nose, mouth, ears, anus, or vagina
- Dizziness
- Drowsiness
- Feelings of agitation
- Feeling unreal or spaced out

- Feeling drunk or inebriated

- Bloating or gut distension

- Excessive gas

- Indigestion or heartburn

- Frequent diarrhea or constipation

- Mucus in stools

- Sugar or carb cravings

- Bad breath or a white tongue

- Blocked salivary glands

- Frequent urinary tract infections, vaginal thrush or vaginosis

- Smelly urine

- Jock itch

- Sexual issues

Again, this list is not exhaustive, but as you can see it is quite extensive. Candida can travel throughout your body can cause symptoms wherever it accumulates leading to potentially widespread unpleasant symptoms.

Is Candida the Only Yeast That Causes Issues?

Candida albicans is the most common yeast present in the human body, but far from the only one. Other yeasts include Candida tropicalis, Candida parapsilosis, and Candida glabrata. In total, there are over 250 strains of Candida, though many of them do not infect or colonize humans, at least to a degree detectable on tests. There are other yeasts outside of the Candida species that can also colonize humans, but these other yeasts comprise less than 10% of the total yeast population in an average person.

The Exposome, Epigenome, and Microbiome

Let's break these down and show how they relate to you, Candida, and your health. The exposome sounds like something crazy from science fiction, but really, it just refers to the collective exposures that we all encounter in our daily lives. This includes toxins in food and water, heavy metals, pesticides, car exhaust, pollen and other allergens, plastics, germs, and so much more. This term is important to know and remember as we will be referencing it throughout the book.

The epigenome is another fancy word that just refers to how our body uses our genetics. Our genetic code is like an architectural diagram for a building. It shows not only how to build a proper, functional building, but also provides alternative designs in case they're needed. The way our body uses these diagrams to adapt to our life and exposome is termed epigenetics. Epigenetics is becoming an increasingly studied field and the varied way that our bodies can adapt using epigenetics is a large reason why humans can overcome all of the varied health challenges that we encounter on a daily basis.

Last up we have the microbiome. This term really encompasses all of the non-human organisms in our body, of which there are a lot. In fact, estimates place the number of non-human cells in our body to be up to 10 times the number of human cells, and what is even crazier is that the genetic and chemical activity has been estimated to be up to 100 times that of our human cells. These facts, which have only been proven and studied within the last 20 years, upend long-standing beliefs about the nature of human beings. In one sense, we are giant living petri dishes brewing all sorts of bacteria, fungi, yeasts, viruses, and parasites, and in another we are humans that at a macroscopic level are aware of none of this. Are we really humans then? Or macrobacteria? Or a bacterial elemental? Or a biological scaffold? Whatever the final decision, it's beyond the scope of this book. This concept though is very important for understanding the role of Candida and how we should approach treating it, as we can't ever eliminate all of it, nor do we want to, as in with healthy humans, we reach a level of homeostasis or balance with the bacteria, viruses, fungi, parasites, and yeasts that live within us. These microbes in our microbiome produce beneficial compounds like vitamins, chemicals, and neurotransmitters that we depend on to be healthy. The goal, then, when treating someone with health issues, is not to kill all the microbes but to figure out where the problems actually are and aid the body in returning to balance.

Another interesting and underappreciated concept related to the microbiome is host influence. Our microbiome produces chemical and electric impulses that are sent from our gut to our brain, and in some cases from the microbes that live in our brain. The impulses influence our choices and behaviors, often without any realization on our part. Intense sugar cravings, avoidance of herbs and vegetables, anxieties and other fears, all can be caused by our microbes. These microbes have an ability called quorum sensing, which is basically a communication network with other microbes of the same type, and once they have a large enough population, or a quorum, they use the newfound power of their large group to start influencing the behavior of the host to improve their lives. *Ophiocordyceps unilateralis*, is an extreme example of this, where this fungus infects ants killing them, the fungus then completely takes over the ant's nervous system, forces them to climb to the top of plants and grasses where the fungus blooms and sends spores out of the ant's head to reproduce. Now, there obviously aren't any microbes that have that substantial of an effect on humans, but Candida in many people can be both a direct and indirect cause of food aversion, mood disorders like anxiety, depression and fear, and the source of intense cravings, especially for sugar or simple carbs that yeasts use as food.

Functional Versus Heroic or Allopathic Medicine, Limitations and Two Core Principles

This concept is so important to understand that an entire book could be dedicated to it. The medical system in the United States and many other countries is considered Heroic or Allopathic, which means that medical professionals treat symptoms and diseases with drugs and surgery. This can be incredibly beneficial for many use cases, like when you're in an accident and need surgery, or have a severe infection and need antibiotics, but what about when you're treating diabetes and other chronic diseases? For that, heroic medicine and most drugs only treat the symptoms rather than the root cause, leaving you chronically sick and taking drugs for life. There are two underlying premises that allopathic medicine is predicated on that have since been proven untrue. The first is Descartes's "Human Machine," where our bodies are a collection of individual parts that function on their own. Our heart, our brain, and our lungs all serve a specific purpose but are entirely interchangeable with organs from another person, and if a single organ is disease or malfunctioning, it's an issue with that organ alone and not indicative of a problem with the organism. It's predominantly for this reason that modern medicine is broken up into specialties as it is. You go to a heart doctor for heart problems, an eye doctor for eye problems, and so forth. Your GP or general physician is supposed to be the doctor tracking it all though, right? But they really aren't. The role of the GP is more to treat common issues like colds and sprains and to evaluate the need for a specialist and send you there, rather than understanding how to treat chronic diseases of those organ systems. This view is at odds with the fundamental interconnectedness of our bodily systems like the nervous, endocrine, and vascular systems. There is constant communication and signaling that happens continuously between all of these organ systems. The multi-step collaboration of various systems allows them to enact complex functions like digestion, without which no complex creature could live.

The second of these premises that is not generally true or only part of the story is Pasteur's concept of "Germ Theory" where a single microbe is responsible for a single illness. In some cases, this is true, like when you get rabies from an animal infected with the rabies virus, but in the majority of cases of health issues and chronic disease, this doesn't hold true. One hundred human beings can be exposed to the same bacteria or virus, and depending on their microbiome, nutrient levels, stress, and many other factors, some will get sick, and some won't. Further complicating that, many humans harbor microbes and pathogens in every tissue in their body. Not just tiny viruses but even entire fungal structures have been found intact inside neurons, with little or no immune response. This concept again could have an entire book written about it, but the takeaway here is that germs, even bad ones, commonly occur in all humans. Even *Yersinia pestis,* the bacteria that caused the Black Plague, is frequently found in random stool tests, indicating persistent human exposure, and yet there are no large outbreaks of the Black Plague in modern times.

It's for that reason that naturopathic, integrative, holistic, eastern, and functional medicine are making a comeback. These approaches, while not all the same, view patients as a whole and try to uncover the root cause or causes, and address those to restore the patient to health and keep them there.

Fundamentals of Autoimmunity

We are just going to do a quick overview of the fundamentals in this book and how they relate to Candida. These concepts represent both the chicken and the eggs of autoimmune dysfunction and Candida can contribute to them, while also having Candida issues resulting from other autoimmune issues. Each of these concepts and areas of autoimmunity can individually or together cause disease, including autoimmune disease, and can also occur as a result of disease and autoimmune disease. Like dominos, one falling interacts with another and continues that cycle, which is what leads to the common belief among most doctors and patients that autoimmune diseases are incurable. It's not that they are incurable, it's that they are complex, with many pillars supporting the disease state, and picking up each domino is harder than letting it fall, and you need to address all those pillars to move out of the disease state and not keep knocking down more dominos.

Candida ties directly into many of these pillars. Mitochondrial dysfunction reduces available energy that your body uses for internal maintenance and repair, which allows candida to grow unchecked. Chronic inflammation of the gut triggers Candida to morph into a more virulent and invasive form that perpetuates the leaky gut. Hormonal issues can module the immune system allowing more candida to grow unchecked. Gut dysfunction and leaky gut allow the translocation of Candida from the gut to the blood, allowing the Candida to spread systemically. Dysbiosis disrupts the natural balance and homeostasis that the microbiome follows, which leads to the overgrowth of fast-growing organisms like Candida. These issues also feed into one another like dominos as mentioned above, where the mitochondrial dysfunction, leads to dysbiosis, leading to leaky gut, leading to chronic inflammation leading to issues with hormone issues, and so on in a vicious cycle. We are here to address some of these pillars by reducing Candida, and restoring health, which for many is enough to substantially reduce or eliminate autoimmunity.

Vagus Nerve Function and Stress

You know those giant undersea cables that connect the internet from various continents so we can all talk to one another? That's basically what the vagus nerve is in the body. It's a giant nerve that extends from the brain and connects to every major organ. It's bidirectional, so stuff happening in your gut transmits up to your brain, like that feeling of butterflies in your stomach, or that fevered rush after eating something spicy, but also sends signals down from the brain to control and regulate organ function based on your interactions with the environment. You've probably heard about fight or flight. When you're faced with a scary situation like a bear chasing you, your body shuts off non-essential functions like digestion, and floods your body with glucose and catecholamines to give you energy. Then once you've escaped, it flips the switch back the opposite way, and you go back to digestion, relaxation, and socializing. That's how it works ideally, at least in modern life; we've found ways and devices to keep ourselves always stimulated. Whether it's doomscrolling, watching TV while eating, spending 15 hours a day glued to a computer monitor, and many other modern lifestyle changes, the end result is that it's difficult for our brain and vagus nerve to flip that switch. So, we remain in fight or flight, which doesn't last forever, but we try and keep it fueled with sugar and caffeine to keep the energy rush going, or we burn out and end up in a state of shutdown, similar to animals that play dead. Either way, we aren't getting back to the rest and digest state where our bodies are healing, repairing, digesting, and restoring to keep us healthy. This, in turn, allows the proliferation of Candida and other microbes and a break from the balance and homeostasis that our bodies are trying to maintain. Later in the book we'll address what we can do about this, and how to prevent it from happening again.

How the Gut and Digestion Affect Your Neurotransmitters and Mood

Our brains are incredibly complex, requiring billions of chemicals and electrical impulses to work properly. Those impulses require and depend on neurotransmitters, which are special chemicals that carry messages between neurons. Most of these neurotransmitters, like dopamine, serotonin, GABA, and norepinephrine, are produced in the gut from amino acids, which are, in turn, produced from the breakdown of proteins. An overgrowth of Candida interferes with digestion leaving much of this protein poorly broken down and unusable for the creation of neurotransmitters, and the Candida crowds out many of the bacteria that would be producing these neurotransmitters. The result is not enough neurotransmitters for optimal health, leaving you feeling sad, anxious, fearful, dopey, or even bipolar, manic, or angry. Luckily, this can be treated by reducing Candida and supplementing, at least temporarily, for any missing amino acids, which we will cover in detail in the later chapters.

Diagnosis Via Suspicion vs Testing, and Doing the Cost-benefit Analysis

Who doesn't love some controversy? Lab testing is very helpful but also quite controversial - let's use Lyme testing as an example. Lyme antibody testing is roughly

35-50% sensitive meaning that the antibody test you get from a traditional doctor will accurately diagnose a person with Lyme's disease as having the disease less than 50% of the time. This is further compounded by the presence of over 52 known species of Borrelia, the bacteria that causes Lyme. Many of these species have low immunoreactivity, meaning that the body produces few or infrequent antibodies, so the tests will only show intermittent positivity. This problem isn't just restricted to Lyme, but with many to most infectious diseases. Couple that with what we talked about previously, where healthy patients harbor all sorts of pathogens, and it becomes very difficult to accurately discern, diagnose, and, therefore, treat patients based on these antibody tests.

Another factor is the cost of many of these tests. Labcorp and Quest don't offer broad testing for all species of Borrelia. You'd have to go to a specialty lab like Vibrant or Igenex, where the specialty tests run from several hundred dollars to several thousand dollars per test. You'll need multiple tests to confirm the presence of the pathogen and then its absence post-treatment.

This has led many doctors, especially those in the naturopathic and integrative fields, to develop diagnostic criteria based on symptom clusters that provide a reasonable specificity to different diseases. Standard diagnostic questionnaires, including MSIDS created by Dr. Horowitz, the Mold and Mycotoxin diagnostic by Dr. Stafford, and the IFM's Candida Screening Questionnaire, allow practitioners an easy way to rule out or increase clinical suspicion of a certain disease. These results, along with the patient's health history, exposome, and other serological results, are then used to create a differential diagnosis, which is a list of potential explanations for their symptoms, and then a treatment plan based on the differential that targets the conditions that are highest on the list. This methodology reduces the patient's cost of treatment and keeps in mind the holistic approach to treating the whole body, which is the goal of integrative medicine.

This also should not be misconstrued to say that no testing is necessary. Testing is vital in giving a clinical picture for many diseases. Tests like the comprehensive digestive stool analysis (CDSA), the organic acids test (OAT), and a toxin panel are the bread and butter of many integrative, functional, and holistic practitioners. These tests evaluate a broad range of pathogens and conditions to give an overall picture, similar to the use of the CBC and CMP by a traditional GP. These tests show issues with the gut and other digestive organs, neurotransmitter, vitamin, and mineral imbalances, colonization of pathogens, and whether clients have been exposed to heavy metals, pesticides, and mycotoxins like those produced by Candida and other molds and yeasts. The practitioner can then develop a comprehensive protocol to address one or many issues like Candida that are likely to be at the root of the client's symptoms.

Herbs vs Drugs for Treatment

How many of you readers would believe that herbs and supplements can be as effective or more effective than many pharmaceutical drugs? Or that many pharmaceutical drugs are actually just concentrated herbs and plant extracts? Or even concentrated mycotoxins like CellCept which is used to prevent organ rejection and is a natural compound produced by molds. It's all true. Why, then, do doctors only prescribe drugs? Mostly it's because they just aren't trained in the effects and dosages of commonly used medicinal herbs. Doctors' schooling is already 8 years plus residency, and adding another year or two to study botany and herbal medicine would strain the patience of most humans, even the largely self-sacrificing group of physicians.

In America, there is also a clash between natural medicine and pharmaceutical companies. Pharmaceutical companies and the drugs they create require extensive and incredibly expensive clinical trials (to the tune of hundreds of millions to billions of dollars), and they have to recoup that money and show profit to shareholders. They partially recoup that money by charging high prices for drugs in countries where the populace can afford those costs and partially by maintaining exclusivity via a variety of means on what doctors can actually prescribe for illnesses. This can lead to a lot of confusion for patients as they usually don't understand all of the forces and interests that are involved, the amount of knowledge required to learn about herbal medicine is high and usually beyond the ability or desire of those who are ill, and due to the cost mentioned before, herbal medicines, even those with thousands of years of use, don't have the high-quality trial data that's used by government agencies to declare a drug or herb fit to be used as medicine. As a result, we, as clients and patients, lose out on available treatment options for common and very treatable conditions. This is important for Candida because there are prescription drugs that can be used, like Nystatin and Diflucan, but also many herbal antifungals, like thyme and oregano, that are just as effective, cheaper, and safer for long-term use. We'll dive into more of those antifungals for treatment later in this book.

Detox vs Disease Treatment

Are you reading this because you feel toxic? Sick? Unwell? It's a good choice, but toxicity doesn't always mean disease. Sure, they're related, but toxicity is really just the accumulation of toxins, either those that are difficult to clear by the body like plastics, or you are accumulating so many that your body can't detoxify fast enough to keep up with the onslaught. Candida and many other molds and yeasts have byproducts of their metabolism, some of which can be toxic to humans. We call these mycotoxins, of which there are many types, with some of the more common ones from Candida being aflatoxin and gliotoxin. When you are getting exposed to toxins in your food, from the chemicals in your house, from chemicals in the air, and are producing them inside your body from your microbiome, it can be difficult to keep the body clear and healthy, leading to disease.

Detoxification, then, is interventions, behaviors, and supplements that help your body eliminate all these toxins from your exposome and stay healthy.

Disease is the breakdown of normal bodily function, health, and resilience. It can happen for many reasons, such as the accumulation of toxins and failure of the body to detox from them, along with other causes like the pillars of autoimmunity that we addressed earlier.

What's interesting is that toxicity can cause disease and disease can cause toxicity, one of those self-perpetuating, vicious cycles of disease and autoimmunity that we addressed earlier. Later in the book we'll tackle how we can more effectively detox, and how this can improve your symptoms and Candida burden.

Food Pyramid Lies –

It seems totally reasonable to have sugar every day, right? No way! In fact, carbohydrates as a broad group are not required for human health. This is one of the big misunderstandings of our time. Our bodies can use either carbohydrates or fats (ketones) for fuel. There are certainly times when one or the other energy source would be preferential, but in general, carbs and carb-containing foods are not required, and it's the consumption or overconsumption of carb-laden foods that lead to many of the issues with Candida, and other dysbiosis, that trouble people's digestive systems across the world.

Principles of Titration

Prepare yourself for another shock. Do you know the dosing of drugs and the recommended dose of supplements? They are generally based on appropriate dosing for a 150-pound man. If you happen to be a man around 150 lbs, that's great! It means that, in most cases, that dosage is a good one for you, but what if you are a woman? Or much lighter or heavier? Or your illness or Candida burden is much less or much more than usual? This is where we introduce titration. It's an incredibly important way to view medicine and supplements because it empowers the patients to take responsibility for their health and work with their providers to move toward the most appropriate and effective dosage to treat them.

Basically, there are the recommended dosages of supplements, which are based on trial data as to what amount is usually effective for the primary use of that supplement, think B vitamins to correct a deficiency of B vitamins. These dosage recommendations are more legalese than medical advice, as the dosing has to be set to something that has at least some chance of being effective while also erring on the side of caution to avoid side effects and potential liability for the supplement manufacturers. That doesn't mean that the dosage on the bottle is what is most appropriate and effective for you. Your physician, as part of your evaluation and treatment, can change the dosage, timing, and frequency to maximize the efficacy of your treatment, and its incumbent on you to give them feedback on how the dosage is affecting you so that they can make continual refinements until you are healthy.

Google Can't Cure You!

Nor should you expect it to. Human health is a complex topic, and most doctors are trained for at least 8 years in medical school, followed by 3-5 more years of training in residency, and for some, another round of training in fellowship. Part of this training is to evaluate symptoms in the context of medical history, to come up with a list of most likely explanations or causes for what's wrong and build a treatment plan to address that list. Googling a symptom or two and expecting to arrive at the best results and what the most effective treatment would be is not a reasonable belief. There are so many symptoms and diseases out there that random googling is not likely to lead you down the right rabbit hole and can lead to lots of wasted time, or even causing harm to yourself by trying supplements or medications that aren't suited to the issues you're dealing with. I know it can be frustrating, and there are many groups that rally against doctors in this day and age, but they are there to help and trained to do so. If a doctor can't help, or you don't feel heard, then fire them and find a doctor who will. They are out there and plenty of organizations like the Institute of Functional Medicine (ifm.org) have lists of holistic and functional medicine doctors and practitioners that treat root causes and chronic conditions.

Chapter 2: How did this happen to me?

"It all began with a seemingly harmless decision to take antibiotics for a lingering cold. For Emily, a busy mom juggling the demands of her career and family, the meds promised quick relief and a return to health. However, her choice unfortunately set off a chain reaction that would begin to unravel her life. The antibiotics, intended to fight off the cold, inadvertently wiped out her gut, paving the way for an overgrowth of Candida. This yeast, usually kept in check by a balanced microbiome, flourished unchecked, leading to a host of debilitating symptoms. Emily's once vibrant energy and bubbly personality waned, replaced by chronic fatigue, brain fog, and a cascade of physical ailments. Her health deteriorated rapidly, leaving her in a state of confusion and despair as she watched her life fall apart, desperate for answers and a path to reclaim her former self. It was only after she reached out and began a Candida detox program that things turned around, and she began to regain the life she thought she had lost forever."

How many of you have a similar story? I certainly did. Most people don't realize that antibiotics can disrupt the microbiome for months, years, or even permanently, even from a single dose. It's so important to take charge of your life and your health and not just rely on a doctor or drug to cure all your issues magically. Part of that "taking charge" is learning how and why people get Candida. Let's take a look at that now.

Why Do Most People Get Candida?

1. **Antibiotics –** Far and away, the most common cause of candidiasis, or a Candida overgrowth, is antibiotics. We are talking about prescription antibiotics for an illness, as well as antibiotics for acne and other chronic issues, as well as antibiotics in meats, other foods, and those that leak into the water supply. Some of these, like using antibiotics for common colds and other non-life-threatening issues, we can cut back on. Others, like the antibiotics in our food supply, we can shift to organic, antibiotic-free foods. For the antibiotics present in the water supply, you can install your water filters in your home to reduce your exposure, whether that is a countertop filter or a whole home water filter, as both can reduce your exposure. You can also check the water quality report that your state or municipality produces, usually every year. If the water quality is deficient and contains high levels of antibiotics or metals and toxins that we'll talk about below, you can call your local politicians to prioritize water improvement projects.

2. **Immune depletion or deficiency –** There are many potential causes of issues with the immune system, from diabetes or other chronic disease to

stress, genetics, and nutrient deficiencies. Chronic diseases can overwhelm the immune system, over time reducing its ability to fight back not just against that disease but against all diseases and invaders. This is commonly seen in patients with gut issues with a depletion of secretory IgA which is an immune cell that is typically plentiful in the gut and helps regulate the microbiome. In those with long-term chronic diseases, the secretory IgA levels will often be very low, indicating that the gut has been overwhelmed and can no longer do a good job of fighting back. This will lead to dysbiosis, overgrowth of bacteria and Candida, reactivation of viruses, and many other unpleasant side effects.

Stress is another factor that can impair the immune system. Chronic stress can impair the production of cortisol and prevent our body from using our vagus nerve to relax from "fight or flight" into "rest and digest." Cortisol impairment directly impacts the immune system's ability to regulate the microbiome and causes blood sugar dysregulation that can further exacerbate Candida overgrowth. The vagus nerve disruption prevents the body from resting properly and fully digesting your food leading to nutrient deficiencies, dysbiosis, and a lack of generalized repair of the body, exacerbating other underlying conditions or diseases.

Genetics can also play a role as there are numerous SNP's or single nucleotide polymorphisms, just minor genetic differences, that can change how our body and immune systems work. Some of these common changes affect methylation, which is how your body turns on and off different genetic sequences to respond and adapt to its environment. Poor methylation can cause issues with immune system function that can lead to the overgrowth or loss of commensalism with candida.

3. **Cortisol issues** – Cortisol is an endocrine hormone that helps the body balance energy, mood, inflammation, metabolism, and the sleep-wake cycle. Imbalances leading to high and very low cortisol levels are detrimental to the body and can lead to microbiome disruption, Candida issues, and other symptoms. Many factors, including chronic stress, illness, and steroid medications like hydrocortisone, can cause these cortisol imbalances.

4. **Sugar and refined carbs** – One of the most common and consistent causes of Candida overgrowth is a diet high in refined carbohydrates and sugars. Refined carbohydrates include foods like bread, chips, and pizza. Sugars include the regular culprits like candy and soda and condiments like ketchup, smoothies, nut butter, and salad dressings. High-sugar fruits like apples, bananas, and grapes are included in this and can cause Candida overgrowth without any of the refined carbs or candy.

5. **Toxins – molds, metals, chemicals.** A broad category that includes environmental toxins like pesticides and plastics, as well as heavy metals like mercury and aluminum, as well as toxins from fungi, including candida, which are called mycotoxins. These toxins, as a group, can interfere with every organ system and function in your body. In fact, the most common symptoms of Candida are not caused by the growth or overgrowth of the

31

Candida itself causing a UTI or similar issue but rather by strains of Candida that produce mycotoxins like aflatoxin and gliotoxin. Your body tries to eliminate these toxins naturally, but if you have a high Candida burden, they can accumulate and require special treatment protocols to detox and restore your health. We'll go over how to detox from these later in the book.

6. **Chlorinated water** – Unbeknownst to many, chlorine is a potent antibiotic and is used for that purpose to keep pools sanitary. When we swim in those pools, we absorb the chlorine through our skin, and orally if we swallow any water. Like the antibiotics we already talked about earlier, chlorine then causes widespread and long-lasting damage to the microbiome that allows Candida to flourish and the body to lose its ability to regulate and keep Candida in a commensal state.

7. **Alcohol** – While this might be unpopular for many to hear, it's essential to know that alcohol damages the gut leading to dysbiosis, Candida overgrowth, and so on. Mixing the alcohol with sugary drinks like Coca-Cola or indulging in wine coolers, margaritas, or other high sugar cocktails only increases that effect. Candida issues are incredibly prevalent in those that drink frequently, and it's nearly impossible to recover if you continue to drink. Many programs exist like AA and others to help reduce alcohol consumption and deal with the physical, spiritual, and social problems that can arise.

8. **Meal spacing** – To move food through the gut, the body has a system called the migratory motor complex, which is a series of electrical waves

that move through the gut, causing a series of contractions that push the food from your stomach down to the colon. This looks sort of like a worm moving where it contracts together and then springs apart. These electrical waves start 2-3 hours after you last ate, depending on the person, what they ate, and some other factors, and will stop again whenever you ingest new calories. Therefore, if you are eating throughout the day, even small snacks, then your MMC will not work properly and food will back up in areas of the small intestine where it shouldn't and you will start growing bacteria and fungi like Candida in the small intestine, leading to a syndrome called SIBO or SIFO which stands for small intestinal bacterial (or fungal) overgrowth.

As we just covered, there are many ways to cause or contribute to Candida getting out of control. It's not surprising that issues from Candida overgrowth and loss of commensalism are so prevalent in modern life. It's not all bad news, though. In the next chapter, we will begin laying out the plan for fighting back, reducing your systems, and restoring your health.

Another important detail to know is that Candida infections present differently in people, and part of that is due to gender and age. Below we cover what a typical symptom profile will look like for female clients, male, and children, and we include a questionnaire afterwards that you can fill out and get a score that shows the likelihood of Candida being a core or root cause of the issues you are facing.

What Does a Typical Female Candida Patient Look Like?

History of oral contraceptives, hormone replacement, persistent vaginal thrush, antibiotic use, experiences painful intercourse or avoids it, frequently consumes high sugar foods and beverages like chocolate, ice cream, soda, crackers, chips, cookies, bread, bananas, oranges, figs, or dried fruit. Loves wine and soft or moldy cheeses. History of GI issues. History of mood issues like anxiety, depression, lack of motivation, or apathy.

What Does a Typical Male Candida Patient Look Like?

Frequently burps or passes gas. Snacks on chips, pretzels, sweets, beer, or mixed drinks, especially if they crave alcohol. Has a wife or girlfriend with yeast or mold issues. Recurrent GI problems like IBS, diarrhea, constipation, bloating or heartburn. History of psoriasis or prostatitis. Issues with motivation, anxiety, and depression.

What Does a Typical Child Candida Patient Look Like?

History of antibiotic use or steroid use like asthma inhalers. Constantly eating or demanding sweet foods, fruits, and simple carbs like bread and crackers. Complaints frequently about tummy pain, pain, or urgency when peeing, or has frequent ear, nose, or throat issues or infections. Was not breast fed. Has terrible mood or behavioral issues that seem unrelated to the situation.

What Kind of Testing Can be Done to Diagnose Candida?

There are tests you can get from your general practitioner, but those tests are primarily geared towards evaluating serious or life-threatening cases like those that occur in cancer, HIV, and otherwise immunocompromised patients. These tests include blood antibody testing and urine testing for a UTI.

Several functional medicine tests can be run as well. The main one is a CDSA (comprehensive digestive stool analysis) which analyzes a stool specimen for all the bacteria, fungi, yeasts, parasites, and viruses contained within. This can give much more accurate data as to the level of candida and the specific species present in the gut. This test is expensive, but along with an OAT (organic acids test), and a toxin test, are part of the "Core 3" tests of functional medicine providers.

The OAT, as mentioned above, is a urine test that measures markers of metabolic health. In patients with high levels of Candida, there are typical profiles, or sets of markers like arabinose, B vitamins, neurotransmitter metabolites, and others that will be off if there is an overgrowth of Candida. The OAT test, in addition to the CDSA, can provide a very high level of certainty as to Candida being the cause or a primary culprit in your health issues.

The last test I mentioned, the toxin test, refers to a test that measures your levels of toxins including mycotoxins, or those from molds and yeasts like Candida, as well as toxins like heavy metals and environmental toxins like plastics and pesticides.

In addition to testing, many functional and holistic health providers use questionnaires as part of the client history and intake to get a rough idea of how likely it is that different pathogens contribute to their issues. We've mentioned the MSIDS and Mold and Mycotoxin questionnaires and below we are going to introduce the Candida Questionnaire, which can give you and your provider a good idea of whether or not Candida is or is one of the root causes of the issues that you're dealing with. Go ahead and read through the questions, writing down your scores from each, and comparing the total to the ranges at the end. If the score is on the lower side, it doesn't rule out Candida, but it's less likely and you will want to do the MSIDS, and Mycotoxin questionnaires available online. If your score is in the middle to high side, it is increasingly likely that Candida is a major player in your health issues. In addition to reading this book, it's important to find a provider with experience in treating Candida to help you on your journey back to health.

Candida Questionnaire

Questionnaires are meant to give you and your health care provider a level of clinical suspicion of pathological levels of Candida. The below questionnaire is based on available questionnaires for Candida. It has two sections and a scoring guide.

Candida Questionnaire (part 1)

HISTORY QUESTION	SCORE
How many times have you taken antibiotics in the past 10 years?	x20 pts each
In the last 10 years have you taken an antibiotic for longer than 1 month?	50 pts
Have you ever had suspicion or been diagnosed with prostatitis, vaginitis, UTI or yeast infection? 20 pts	20 pts
Have you been pregnant? 3 for 1, 5 for 2+	3 for 1, 5 for 2+
Have you taken birth control pills?	<2 yrs 10 pts, >2 yrs 20 pts
Have you taken a steroid like hydrocortisone either orally or inhaled?	10 pts + 1 pt per use
Are you sensitive to pesticides, perfumes, fabrics, or other chemicals?	Mild 5 pts, Mod-severe 20 pts
Do warm, damp places or mold exposure make your symptoms worse?	20 pts
Have you suspected or been diagnosed with athlete's foot, jock itch, ringworm, or fungal infections of the skin or nails?	20 pts
Do you crave sugar, breads or alcoholic beverages?	10 pts each

Candida Questionnaire (part 2)

Go through the symptoms list below and circle which you have. Then give a score of 3 for each mild symptom, 6 for each moderate symptom, and 9 for each severe symptom.

Fatigue unrelated to exercise, Poor memory, Feeling spacey, Indecisive, Numbness burning or tingling, Insomnia, Muscle aches and pains, Joint pain or swelling, Muscle weakness, Abdominal pain, Bloating, Constipation, Diarrhea, Vaginal burning, itching, or discharge
Prostatitis, Impotence, Low libido, Endometriosis, Menstrual irregularities
Anxiety, Sadness, Cold hands or feet, Shaking and irritability when hungry
Drowsiness, Lack of coordination, Mood swings, Headaches, Balance issues
Ear pressure, Chronic rashes or itching, Bruise easily, Psoriasis , Indigestion or heartburn
Food sensitivities, Mucus in stools, Itchy anus, Dry mouth or throat, Rash or blisters in mouth
Bad breath or halitosis, Persistent body odor, Nasal congestion

Scoring

MEN	WOMEN	INTERPRETATION
Less than 50	Less than 60	Yeast is less likely to cause health problems
51-100	61-120	Yeast-connected health problems are possibly present
101-150	121-180	Yeast-connected health problems are probably present
Over 150	Over 180	Yeast-connected health problems are very likely present

Chapter 3: Phase 1 - Calming the Storm

Reducing inflammation and symptoms caused by Candida overgrowth is a journey that begins with addressing the root causes of digestive imbalance. Supplements such as digestive enzymes, Betaine HCL, glutamine, licorice root, zinc carnosine, and marshmallow root are pivotal in restoring gut health by improving digestion, reducing inflammation, and healing the intestinal lining. Complementing this supplement regimen with a targeted healing diet like GAPS, SCD, FODMAP, Paleo, or Carnivore diet will reduce inflammation, correct digestive imbalance and many nutrient deficiencies, boost the immune system, and lower the levels of Candida in your body. All of these diets focus on eliminating inflammatory foods and introducing nutrient-dense, easily digestible options that nourish the body and promote a balanced microbiome. They differ slightly in method, some having stages and start off very restricted, adding new foods and food groups over time, and others go right into eating the core diet immediately. There are benefits and drawbacks to doing it both ways, and part of this process is to empower you to choose the diet that you believe you can accommodate daily for the next 3 to 6 months, as that's how long phases 1 and 2 of this protocol will last. Ideally, you'll continue with the diet for longer as it will help with Phase 4, which is bolstering your body so that you won't need to come back to this book again in a couple of months or years and have to redo the protocols because you celebrated completion by eating a chocolate cake every day. Not saying you will, but some clients have literally done exactly that, and I know from personal experience how tempting it can be, once you are feeling good and forget the pain of being sick, to abandon the good habits you've set up and go back to what you used to do, but DON'T DO IT. Maintain the disciple, adopt the identity level change that you are a healthy human being with healthy habits and diet, and you deserve to be healthy and not on the couch with cramps because you ate something that you know you shouldn't have. So, let's talk more in-depth about these diets and give you the information you need to pick one.

Step 1: Pick and Start a Healing Diet

The most important part of this process and protocol is picking a diet that you can do and adhere to for the duration of the protocol. Some of these diets can be tough, some tougher than others, and different people will do better both in terms of discipline and with symptoms on different diets. It can't be stressed enough, though, that adherence to a healing diet can make or break the entire protocol because the food you eat is the food that will be given to your Candida. If you are eating sugars and simple carbs, it will feed the Candida, and the Candida will not go away no matter how many other steps you adhere to. Will the other steps help reduce symptoms? Absolutely, but I have not seen or heard of any clients who continued eating something like the standard American diet that got better and stayed healthy.

Unlike many of the Candida protocols out there, we did not create a special diet, to tout as the next big thing. The healing diets included below are time tested and broadly used for healing dysbiosis and disease by millions of people. They have scientific backing, plenty of literature, case studies, testimonials, Facebook and Reddit support groups, and more cookbooks and YouTube channels than you can shake a stick at. This was done intentionally to give you a choice, where all the choices are healthy and good, and get you connected to other people going through what you are in those social groups, rather than using this book to sell you a special Candida diet cookbook.

The diets that are part of this protocol include the gut and psychology syndrome diet (GAPS), the specific carbohydrate diet (SCD), the Paleo and Autoimmune Paleo diet (AIP), the fermentable oligo, di, monosaccharide, and polyol diet (FODMAP), and the Carnivore diet. All of these are well documented in their ability to heal disease broadly, but also specifically to help the microbiome and reduce Candida. Review the charts below, watch some YouTube videos, read some sample menus for each on the internet to get a feel for which one calls to you and commit to it, for at least the next 3-6 months while you complete this protocol and all of its steps.

If you need a recommendation because this is all too overwhelming, or whatever the reason, Paleo is the diet for you. It has the most scientific backing, the highest-quality literature, and the biggest support groups, so you'll be able to commiserate with others on your journey.

Paleo Diet

FOODS TO INCLUDE	FOODS TO AVOID
Vegetables	Refined, processed foods
Fruits (fresh fruit, natural dried fruit)	Sugars and sugar-sweetened beverages
Eggs	Grains
Nuts and seeds	Dairy
Grass-fed beef, wild-caught fish, and poultry	Legumes (beans and peanuts)
Unrefined oils like coconut, olive, and avocado	Refined vegetable oils, seed oils

GAPS Diet

FOODS TO INCLUDE	FOODS TO AVOID
Homemade bone broth	Processed and packaged foods
Probiotic-rich fermented foods like sauerkraut and kefir	Grains and gluten-containing products
Non-starchy vegetables	Sugar and artificial additives
Healthy fats like coconut oil and olive oil	Starchy vegetables
Wild-caught fish, organic meats & eggs	Coffee, Alcohol (occasional okay)
Fresh fruits in moderation	All beans except green and white navy beans
Fermented organic dairy, if tolerated	Conventional and non-fermented dairy

FODMAP Diet

FOODS TO INCLUDE	FOODS TO AVOID
Vegetables: carrot, cucumber, lettuce, eggplant, celery, green beans, squash	Vegetables: asparagus, cauliflower, artichoke, green peas, onion, garlic
Fruits: cantaloupe, kiwi, orange, blueberry, pineapple	Fruits: apples, peaches, pears, plums, watermelon, dried fruit, juices
Almond milk, some cheeses like feta, kefir	Cow's milk, yogurt, cottage cheese
Proteins: eggs, grass-fed beef, wild-caught fish, and poultry	Legumes, some processed meats
Gluten-free and ancient grains	Gluten
Pumpkin seeds, walnuts, peanuts, macadamia nuts	Cashews, pistachios
Dark chocolate, maple syrup	Artificial sweeteners, honey, high fructose corn syrup

SCD Diet

FOODS TO INCLUDE	FOODS TO AVOID
Vegetables: Asparagus, celery, zucchini, greens, beets, broccoli, tomatoes, squash	Vegetables: Cucumbers, potatoes, sweet potatoes, canned vegetables
Most fruits	Soy products
Butter, some cheeses, homemade yogurt	Soft cheeses, margaine, sour cream
Eggs, grass-fed beef, wild-caught fish, and poultry	Processed and canned meats
Most nuts, seeds and beans	All grains and gluten
Honey	All other sweeteners
Other: most herbs/spices, most cooking oils, most juices, non-dairy milks	Other: aloe vera, protein powder, chlorella, hemp seed/protein, spirulina

Carnivore Diet

FOODS TO INCLUDE	FOODS TO AVOID
Grass-fed beef, wild-caught fish, poultry, pork, and wild game	Grains & starches; even meats with breading or any added ingredients
Eggs	Sugars and sugar-sweetened beverages
Butter, ghee, lard, tallow	Seed oils, olive oil, avocado oil, coconut oil, plant-based fats
Cheese, heavy cream, raw milk in moderation	Most dairy aside from the exceptions to the left
Salt	Nuts, seeds, legumes
Bone broth	Vegetables & fruits

Diets for Candida Detox

DIET	DISTINGUISHING FEATURES
Paleo/AIP	Focuses on eating similarly to what our ancestors ate and avoiding processed and refined foods. Balances blood sugar levels and denies Candida the refined carbs it needs to thrive.
FODMAP	Aims to eliminate short-chain carbohydrates in the diet that can be difficult to digest and feed Candida and harmful bacteria
GAPS	Looks for nutrients that aid in immune system and gut functionality and restoration. Places emphasis on fermented foods and bone broth to heal the gut thus promoting long-term Candida balance in the body.
SCD	Eliminates carbohydrates with the exception of foods mostly composed of monosaccharides, which are simple carbohydrates and are easy to digest. Aims to restore a balance of beneficial bacteria in the gut.
Body Ecology	Aims to restore gut health and the microbiome of the body by replenishing good bacteria in the digestive tract and strengthening the immune system.
Carnivore	Goal is to eat only animal products, which puts the body into a state of ketosis. The lack of carbs and sugars helps to drastically reduce the population of Candida.

THE FAST LANE or extra credit for the nerds out there like me – is as you might have guessed, FASTING. Fasting is the fastest way to reduce issues with the microbiome and would be done in addition to the other protocols and the healing diet. Fasting would then be introduced intermittently to speed the process, because when you fast, your body, your metabolism, immune system, and nervous system don't have to deal with the constant influx of food that it has to process, and all of the bugs and toxins that come along with it. Instead, your body gets to focus on housekeeping, which includes getting rid of any pests like Candida, that are around. Fasting has been used for that purpose, for detoxification and purification, especially in spiritual and religious practices for the entirety of recorded human history, and likely even longer.

Now, I'll be the first to tell you that fasting is not easy, that's why this part is extra credit, and the bonus is that it can improve a lot of other health and longevity markers, far more than just improving Candida, but it takes discipline and determination. It's also not for everyone as young children, pregnant women, those with a BMI of 16 or below, and those with an unstable medical condition should not try fasting, and those that do so should do so under the guidance of their physician.

There are some more things to know about fasting like what breaks a fast, which is just about anything that stimulates the digestive system, which for most people is anything other than water and electrolytes. That means no food of any kind, no 0-calorie foods, no sodas, no sparkling waters, no gum, no nothing, just water and electrolytes. And electrolytes are important as your body still needs those for your muscles and nerves to function, and not just a small pinch of salt, as your body needs 2-3 grams per day if you aren't exercising, and 3-4 grams per day if you are. Make sure the salt doesn't contain any other additives as well like sugar as there are some sketchy supermarket brands out there with added ingredients.

The timing of your fasting is also important. Most new clients will do a fasting pyramid, where they start with a single day or 24 hours of fasting beginning one evening after dinner and lasting until dinner the next day. This usually results in the least amount of sleep disruption due to hunger, as you'll still have food in your stomach overnight. The duration is then increased as your body gets used to the stress of fasting and reworks some of your metabolism and epigenetics to accommodate so that the second fast will usually be 36-48 hours, with at least a full week break in between fasts. This range is what many long-term fasters tend to be able to accommodate on a weekly basis, somewhere between 1-2 days of fasting per week, which might seem like a lot until you realize that the longest fast on record is 382 days, during which the man, Angus Barbieri, lost 276 lbs. For many of you reading, weight loss might be a blessing, and fasting is the fastest way to do so and keep it off. But there are risks, including cardiac issues if you don't take the recommended electrolytes and don't have adequate protein intake during the periods of non-fasting. Ultimately, it's up to you if you want to shoot for extra credit and incorporate fasting but the information is here to support you.

Step 2: Putting Out the Fire

Candida overgrowth can cause many unpleasant symptoms and interfere significantly with digestion, but it doesn't necessarily affect everyone equally. The vast majority of clients with Candida have GI issues from constipation, diarrhea, IBS, and so on, and for those people, these supplements will be incredibly beneficial and piggyback on the benefits of the healing diet. For those with good gut health, who have a type 3 – 5 stool on the Bristol chart at least once a day, first, congratulations! There are fewer of you than you think. Second, you don't necessarily need these supplements. You can test them to see if they help you feel better, or if you know on holidays you'll cheat on the healing diet and want to protect yourself from as much damage as possible, you can keep some in your back pocket. Everyone else, though, will need some of these supplements and to implement the activities below to improve their digestion. There are also follow-on sections with supplements that help directly with mast cell issues, which are common in those with Candida and gut issues, as well as options for people with neurological or psychological symptoms. Similar to the gut supplements, we view these as optional for clients who don't have the related symptoms. There's no need to fix something that isn't broken.

Gut supplements:

- Aloe vera
- Glutamine
- Deglycyrrhizinated Licorice Root (DGL)
- Marshmallow root
- Zinc and zinc carnosine
- Omega-3's

Additional anti-inflammatories that are not gut-specific include:

- Curcumin
- S-adenosylmethionine
- Boswellia serrata or Frankincense
- Uncaria or Cat's Claw (do not use if you have Lupus)

Activities that can also reduce inflammation include:

- Exercise
- Yoga
- Biofeedback

- Frequency specific microcurrent (FSM)

- Massage

- Cold exposure

- Grounding

Combining these anti-inflammatory supplements and activities should drastically reduce the frequency and intensity of systems. In combination with the protocols, we will go over in the next chapter, many clients experience rapid improvement, some in as little as 12 to 24 hours.

Step 2a: Options for Mast Cell Issues

Mast cells are an important part of your immune system. These cells are present in connective tissue throughout the body but are especially prevalent in the gut. Gut issues, especially leaky gut or intestinal hyperpermeability, allow food and bacteria to migrate through the gut wall into the blood and contact these mast cells. The mast cells then release histamine and other inflammatory mediators to try and fix the issue. This is a major contributor to both "allergies" and food sensitivities because the histamine release can present both with common allergy-type symptoms of stuffy or runny nose, red or itchy eyes, congestion, hoarseness, asthma, but also symptoms more associated with illness and disease like chronic headaches, diarrhea, rash or hives, low blood pressure, and even heart issues.

Candida can disrupt the gut in a big way leading to leaky gut and issues with histamine and mast cells. Luckily, there are a few supplements in our arsenal that can help reduce the histamine symptoms while we address the root cause. Some of these supplements include:

- Vitamin C

- Quercetin

- Bromelain

- Stinging Nettle

- Ginger

- Thyme

Over-the-counter antihistamines can also be used but should be viewed as a last resort due to side effects and potential health complications from long-term use. Examples of these antihistamines would include:

- Loratadine (Claritin)

- Cetirizine (Zyrtec)

- Desloratadine (Clarinex)

- Fexofenadine (Allegra)

Keep in mind that the use of antihistamine drugs should be only on a temporary and as needed basis while the underlying cause of candidiasis and gut issues are being resolved.

Step 2b: Options for Neuropsychiatric issues

Many clients with Candida and other digestive issues will have issues with mood like anxiety, depression, excess stress, anger, and agitation that they deal with on a frequent basis. Part of this can be attributed to poor digestion, which robs the body of essential nutrients like amino acids that are used to make neurotransmitters like dopamine and GABA. For these clients, there are several complementary options that can be explored to improve their symptoms and quality of life without having to rely on prescription medications. One of the most effective therapies for these clients is amino acid therapy, where specific amino acids are supplemented based on the specific mood issues they are dealing with. The chart below has specific mood issues along with the neurotransmitter associated with those symptoms, and the amino acid that's generally deficient that causes the symptoms.

Amino Acid Therapy Chart (page 1)

SEC. NO.	DEFICIENCY SYMPTOMS	SUBSTANCES CRAVED	NATURAL SOLUTIONS	NEUROTRANS-MITTER PROMOTERS
1	Frequent cravings for sugar, starch, or alcohol Irritable, stressed, shaky if meals are delayed	Sweets Starches Alcohol	L-glutamine 500-1,500 mg x 2-3 early morning, mid morning mid afternoon	**Back-up fuel source for entire brain** makes us feel stable, calm, and balanced
2	Crave pick-me ups from substances in column B Apathetic depression Lack of energy Lack of drive Lack of focus, concentration ADD Easily bored	Caffeine Sweets Starches Chocolate Aspartame Diet pills Cocaine Tobacco Marijuana	L-tyrosine 500-1,500 mg early morning, mid morning	**Catecholamines** arousal energy mental focus drive
3	Overstressed Stiff, tense muscles Hard to relax, get to sleep Overwhelmed and burned out Eat to relieve stress	Sweets Starches Tobacco Maijuana Valium, Xanax Alcohol	GABA 100- 500 mg as often as needed (add relaxing taurine or theanine, if needed)	**GABA** calmness, relaxation sleep, muscle pain relief

Amino Acid Therapy Chart (page 2)

SEC. NO.	DEFICIENCY SYMPTOMS	SUBSTANCES CRAVED	NATURAL SOLUTIONS	NEUROTRANS-MITTER PROMOTERS
4	Very sensitive to emotional (or physical) pain Tear up, cry easily Crave treats for comfort, enjoyment, reward, or numbing "Love" or get a high from foods in column B, drugs, or behaviors such as over exercise, infatuation, self-harm, starving, purging	Sweets Starches Chocolate Exercise Oxycontin Marijuana Alcohol Flour or milk products Fats	DL-phenylalanine (or D-phenylalanine) 500-1,500 mg mid morning mid afternoon	**Endorphins** Emotional & physical pain relief Pleasure Reward Loving feelings Numbness
5	Afternoon or evening cravings Negativity, depression Worry, anxiety, low self-esteem Obsessive thoughts/behaviors Winter blues PMS Irritability, rage Panic, phobias Fibromyalgia, TMJ Hard to get to sleep Insomnia, disturbed sleep Hyperactivity Benefit from SSRIs	Sweets Starches Alcohol Marijuana Ecstasy	5-HTP 50-150 mg mid afternoon and if needed for sleep (by 10 PM); or L-tryptophan 500-1,500 mg mid afternoon and if needed for sleep (by 10 PM) Melatonin 0.5-5 mg for sleep at bedtime (by 10 PM)	**Serotonin** Emotional flexibility Self-confidence Optimism Sense of humor **Melatonin** (made from serotonin) Good sleep

In addition to the amino acids, there are other supplements and interventions that can help as listed below:

- Omega 3's

- Ashwagandha

- Meditation

- Improving sleep quality

- Specific probiotics

- Exercise

Step 3: Cut Out the Bad Stuff

This shouldn't come as a surprise but Candida and most yeasts feed on sugars and other simple carbs. If our goal is to reduce Candida, then we must eliminate sugar and most simple carbs from our diets. The problem is that sugar is everywhere now. It's in condiments and drinks of all kinds, including milk, salad dressing, and even spice mixes. Unfortunately, for most clients, a reduction isn't enough to get the Candida levels low enough to no longer cause issues, and they have to eliminate sugar and simple carbs completely. Keep in mind that all the healing diets from the previous section have their own exclusion lists, and most of those will overlap with this list, but we wanted to list them here as well for clarity and ease of use. Here's an overview of foods that need to be eliminated for the first 3 to 6 months:

- Sugar
- Most fruits (each diet will have its exceptions)
- Soda
- Candy
- Alcohol
- Most processed foods
- Breads (with the possible exception of certain grain-free breads like those using almond or coconut flour)
- Preservatives
- Sweeteners (except for Xylitol and Stevia)

Step 4: Improve Digestion with Supplements and Lifestyle

Digestion and gut health are crucial to feeling better and keeping Candida in check. The following supplements and tips will help improve your digestion and in conjunction with the healing diet and anti-inflammatories, will set you on the track to health.

The two most important supplements for digestion are digestive enzymes and an acid supplement. Acid is the first step of digestion in the stomach and a critical one in the breakdown of proteins. It also helps to keep Candida and other microbes out of the stomach and upper small intestine where they don't belong, as a proper stomach pH with adequate acid is enough to dissolve any bacteria, fungi, or yeasts that would be present. To boost stomach acid, clients typically use a supplement called Betaine HCl, often with additional ingredients like Pepsin to augment the effect.

Enzymes are the other critical ingredient to good digestion. The acid starts the process, and enzymes finish it, breaking the food down into small pieces that our body and microbiome can use. There are many enzyme supplements out there, but you want to go for a full spectrum blend of amylase, protease, and lipase. The specific amounts of each will vary between brands, and the amount of each that you need varies based on what you are eating, but in a broad sense, you need a good amount of each. Technically, carnivore diet eaters will only need protease and lipase as there shouldn't be any carbs for the amylase to break down, but there are not any mainstream enzyme brands marketed for the carnivore diet.

One other class of supplements to keep in mind that improve digestion is bile acids. These bile acids, released by the liver and stored in the gallbladder are used in the digestion of fat. People with Candida issues often have gallbladder and liver issues as well due to the growth of Candida into the small intestine and then into those organs. Supplementation can be appropriate if you have symptoms which can include:

- Light-colored or gray stools

- Very foul-smelling stools

- Floating, sticky, or tar-like stools

- A glossy or fatty sheen in the toilet after defecation

- Pain after eating in the upper right of your chest close to where your ribs start

If any of these symptoms are frequent or consistent, supplementing bile acids, generally in the form of tauroursodeoxycholic acid (TUDCA) would be indicated.

In addition to these supplements and a healing diet, it's crucial to adopt the following behaviors that will help you digest your food.

Other Ways to Improve Digestion:

- Relax and take your time while eating. Rushing will keep your nervous system in fight-or-flight and prevent you from releasing the right amount of stomach acid and digestive enzymes to break the food down. This food will then ferment, leading to an overgrowth of Candida and other microbes.

- Chew your food well, at least 30 times for most foods. You start releasing enzymes in your mouth that break down carbohydrates, and the mechanical grinding of your teeth breaks down food so that the acid and enzymes you release can better reach the nutrients in the food.

- Begin intermittent fasting (IF) or time-restricted feeding (TRF) by narrowing the window of time in which you eat. Many who start this process will begin with a 12-hour window, IE, 6 AM to 6 PM. Over time moving to narrower windows of 10, 8, 6, or even 4 hours in which to eat. The most extreme version of TRF is called OMAD, which stands for one meal a day and has shown to be incredibly beneficial for the people who are able to do it.

- Focus on eating and do not have the TV, computer, or cell phone nearby. These devices stimulate your nervous system and prevent good digestion.

- Eat larger meals earlier, with dinner being the smallest meal. This will help digestion, blood sugar, and the quality of your sleep.

- Smell, taste, and savor your foods. Even if they aren't your favorite foods, taking the time to focus on the flavors and smells will stimulate the release of stomach acid and enzymes to help better digest the food you're eating.

- Some people have issues with raw fruits and vegetables. The fiber in these is incredibly important, but it's even more important for you to digest them properly. To that end, you can juice them, adding back in some pulp if tolerated, and they can also be steamed, grilled, boiled, baked, or stewed to improve digestibility.

- Unlike vegetables, meats are better digested when they are cooked less. Medium rare or medium for beef is ideal. Chicken and pork need to be cooked thoroughly to eliminate pathogens, but not so much that they brown or caramelize. Fish and shellfish should be cooked thoroughly as they can contain virulent pathogens.

- Part of the digestive process includes something called the migrating motor complex (MMC). This complex is how your intestines squeeze the food from your stomach to your colon allowing for processing along the way. The electrical waves that cause this begin 2 to 3 hours after eating and stop whenever more calories via food or drink are detected. Meal spacing is the practice of eating meals more than 3 hours and ideally at least 5 hours apart to allow your MMC to move your food down in an orderly manner.

- Some clients have issues with the MMC and motility either due to improper meal spacing, or due to damage from toxins or other causes. Motility aids, which are supplements that stimulate the MMC, can help move the process along, improving digestion and reducing overgrowth in the small intestine from food staying there too long. Some of these motility aids include:
  - Ginger
  - Fiber like psyllium husk
  - Peppermint oil
  - Medications like metoclopramide, somatostatin, erythromycin, and naloxone

- Another tip that clients have found helpful but has fewer scientific studies is the practice of food combining. The principle here is that certain food combinations require similar amounts of time in the stomach and small intestine and therefore digest better. Below is a chart where the combinations have been worked out for you to try.

Proper Food Combining

Poor

Proteins
Meat
Soaked seeds & nuts

Digestion is more difficult
when proteins and starches are eaten within 3 hours of each other

Starches
Beans
Legumes
(Rice, grains)

Good

Good

All Vegetables
Mix well with either a protein
OR a starch

Poor

Poor

Fruits

Fruits should not follow or be eaten with protein, starch, or vegetables!

Poor

Poor

Acid
Citrus
Pineapples
Pomegranates
Strawberries
Sour fruits

Sub-Acid
Apples
Cherries
Grapes
Mangos
Papayas

Sweet
Bananas
Dried fruit
Pears

BONUS – Dispelling Nutrition Myths:

Before we move on, I wanted to tackle a few myths that you've probably heard from your mom, or neighbor, or government, or coworker, that aren't based on the latest science and can hinder your progress.

The Standard American Diet Supplies all the Nutrients we Need.

This is false. Depending on which nutrient you look at, some to most of the US does not meet the daily requirements. In fact, more than 94% of all Americans do not get their daily requirement of vitamin D.

Our Food Contains "Safe Levels" of Pesticides and Other Chemicals

Again, this is false as recent studies have shown that for many of these pesticides and industrial chemicals, there are no "safe levels" despite the official guidelines put out by the FDA, EPA, and other agencies.

Chlorine, Fluoride, and Other Chemicals in our Water are Harmless

Also, false! Studies have shown that not only are the levels of potentially harmful chemicals higher than the legal limits in many municipal water supplies, such as the lead levels in Flint, Michigan, but many of these chemicals do not have a dosage where they do not cause harm.

Sugar is a Natural Part of the Diet

False, false, false!!! Depending on what source you use, the average American consumes between 60 and 150 lbs of sugar per year. For comparison, 200 years ago, the average sugar intake was less than 5 lbs per year. If we go further back and look at the diets of our ancestors, as they do for diets like Paleo, the average human had less than 1 lb of sugar, and depending on lineage and geographic region, many had close to zero sugar for their entire lives. As you can see, until the modern era, sugar, outside of natural sugars in fruits and berries, was not part of the diet of any human beings. We didn't evolve to eat it, and our microbiomes neither need it nor thrive - at least the healthy microbes don't - from eating it.

Chapter 4: Phase 2 – Cleanse and Detox the Candida

Welcome to what you've all been waiting for: the section where we dive into how to actually kill off the excess Candida and start restoring your health. These protocols have worked for thousands of patients, including myself, and have benefited from years of tweaking, refining, and improvement to maximize efficacy and manage any side effects as best as possible. Many of you will begin to improve very quickly, sometimes in as few as 12 hours, but many will require more time before seeing substantial relief. Many factors affect our health and recovery, and healing is not a nice linear path, often having its ups and downs before you arrive at your health goals. On the bad days, it's important to keep the goal in mind, know that things are and will continue to get better and maintain consistency. On the good days, enjoy your improving health, and maintain consistency. As you might have noticed, consistency is key to detoxing from Candida, restoring your health, and staying healthy.

This road you are about to travel is a long one. Most patients require 3 to 6 months on the protocols before their body has detoxed and healed enough to keep Candida and other pathogens in check on their own. There are, unfortunately, no instant cures, no drugs, even the powerful ones like Amphotericin B, that can eliminate all the Candida and keep it from ever coming back. So, prepare yourself, make sure you have all the supplies and supplements you need, the emotional and social support, and the resolve and clarity of purpose that you want to be healthy, that you are ready to be a new healthy you, and let's do this.

The rest of this chapter will be divided into cleansing protocols and a detox plan. The cleansing will be the supplements and herbs that you will use to kill off the excess Candida, and the detox will be how we eliminate the lipopolysaccharides and other toxins released by the Candida while it's dying.

Here's an overview of what we are going to tackle:

- The core Candida detox protocol that everyone will do
- The supplemental protocols for those who have specific issues with Candida in their nails, genitals, nose, or throat
- Additional treatment options for especially tough or treatment-resistant cases
- Supplements, treatments, and tips for detoxing

The Core Candida Detox and Cleanse Protocol:

The core of this protocol is antifungal herbs that have a strong and proven effect against Candida. There are many other antimicrobial herbs out there that also have some effect, but these specific herbs have shown time and again to be effective against many strains of Candida, have low toxicity, and have much milder side effects compared to drugs like Nystatin.

Antifungals –

- Thyme - great vs drug-resistant candida, mild and low toxicity, dosing of tincture is 0.7ml 1 – 3 times a day
- Oregano oil - very potent but often causes GI distress, dosing 500-1000mg 2-4 times a day
- Pau d'arco – medium effect, low to medium toxicity, makes great tasting tea, dosing is 1-4 cups per day
- Garlic extract – Potent antimicrobial and blood thinner, dosing is 0.7ml of tincture, 2-4 times a day, can also use Allicin extract pills up to 10,000 mcg per day.
- Grapefruit seed extract – potent anti-Candidal herb, dosing is 5 to 15 drops 1 – 3 times a day
- Undecylenic and Caprylic acid combination – each of these are potent anti-Candidals and together they synergize incredibly well. Dosing for caprylic acid is 500 mg twice a day, and for undecylenic acid is 100mg twice a day. Unfortunately, we are not aware of any products on the market that combine

these two. Also, undecylenic acid works best in combination with digestive enzymes and HCL supplements.

This protocol calls for using two of these options at a time to give Candida the one-two punch needed to reduce levels and symptoms. If your symptoms and Candida burden is fairly low, the initial combo would include the milder herbs like garlic and thyme. For tougher cases, undecylenic and caprylic acid is a great combo, and can include grapefruit seed extract for an extra kick that works very well together. For the toughest cases, the two acids, along with Oregano oil should help a great deal. Out of all the herbs listed, Oregano oil has the most side effects in most people, and therefore is reserved for the toughest cases, but it is incredibly potent, and worth trying if some of the milder herbs aren't delivering the results you are looking for.

In addition to the dosing and herb combinations, these herbs are typically used in cycles. For example, in month one, you begin with garlic and thyme, then after six weeks you cycle off those two and begin Pau d'arco and Grapefruit seed for the next six weeks. At the end of cycle two, you evaluate with your practitioner as to whether or not the Candida is cleared sufficiently, or you need another cycle, or a stronger cycle.

If, after four complete cycles, and trying all the listed herbs, and you've been faithfully adhering to the diet and cut out sugars, and you still have symptoms, you need to evaluate whether it's appropriate to look at other root causes to attack your symptoms from another angle, or to try and add prescription antifungals to your regimen.

Sample Supplement Cycle Chart

WEEKS	SUPPLEMENTS
1-6	Thyme 0.7 mL 1-3x/day Garlic 0.7 mL 1-3x/day
7-12	Pau d'arco tea 1-4 cups per day Grapefruit seed extract 5-15 drops, 1-3x/day
13 -18	Evaluate with provider

Prescription Antifungals with their Relative Strength and Toxicity:

These drugs are potent, with great potential for serious side effects, including organ damage, allergic reactions, and even death, and should not be considered unless all other treatment options have failed, or the patient is hospitalized with a progressive, systemic infection. It's unfortunate that due to their frequency of use and use of antifungals in commercial farming and the raising of livestock, many strains of yeast and Candida have become resistant to these medications, similar to how MRSA and other bacteria have become resistant to antibiotics. This means that even when they are needed many of them will no longer have the effect that they are needed for, narrowing down the options for you to get healthy. Regardless, the antifungal drugs listed below are all potent inhibitors of Candida and can be evaluated for use if the herbal protocols fail.

Itraconazole – the weakest effect, moderate toxicity

Nystatin – weak effect, lowest toxicity, but can still cause strong Herx in some patients

Ketaconazole – medium effect, moderate toxicity

Fluconazole – strong effect, moderate toxicity, many fungi are resistant now

Amphotericin B IV – strongest, severe side effects and kidney damage

As stated before, and as can't be stated enough, there are many potentially serious interactions between drugs, and potential side effects of which to be aware. Be sure to let your practitioner know of any other supplements and medications you're on before starting a prescription anti-fungal.

Supplemental Protocols for Specific Candida Issues:

With the main protocol that everyone will do out of the way, we will now tackle the protocols for infections of the male and female genitals, nails, ears, nose and throat. These protocols are intended to be done multiple times. Many clients require seven or more continuous days to clear a local infection of vaginal thrush, so don't feel bad if you aren't cured after the first. Commit to doing these specific protocols as long as is needed while you do the core Candida detox.

There are many ingredients, and in some cases tools like bowls, spools, and applicators are needed. Please read ahead and ensure you have what is needed before going through the steps. You don't want to be in the middle of step 2 and realize you don't have all the ingredients or the right applicator.

Keep in mind that these protocols have evolved over time into what they are based on feedback and healing power as evidenced from thousands of clients. Unless you are trained in holistic or integrative medicine, you should stick with the protocol as listed. It can be tempting to change things up based on something that you've read or a YouTube video you watched, but I implore you to give these a shot and truly believe that the results will speak for themselves.

Most of these specific protocols involve 3 steps, first to kill the Candida, then restore the pH balance and good microbes, and then calm and soothe the affected area. Make sure you are doing all of the steps. Skipping the first will prevent the elimination of Candida, skipping the second will allow the Candida to come back, and skipping the third will leave you with more pain and discomfort than is necessary.

Vaginosis Protocol:

Overview: This protocol will help cleanse the candida and other pathogens in the vaginal area. The douche afterward will help cleanse the area and balance the pH of the vagina, allowing healthy bacteria to grow back.

Supplies: 4 bowls, 3 spoons, manuka honey 15+ UMF, garlic cloves, apple cider vinegar, colloidal silver, 1 quart of plain sugar-free yogurt, and vaginal applicator or turkey baster

1. Combine 2 tsp manuka honey with two freshly chopped or crushed garlic cloves in a bowl

2. Mix and warm by suspending the mix in a larger bowl of warm water

3. In a separate bowl, mix 1 cup water, 3 tbsp of apple cider vinegar and 1 tsp of colloidal silver

4. Lay down and, using the applicator, insert it into the vagina. Spread the paste around the vagina and anus.

5. Leave for at least 20 but not more than 30 minutes.

6. Use a warm douche with the mix of water, ACV and colloidal silver. Use the remaining liquid to wash off the honey outside the vagina.

7. (Optional) If you are experiencing pain or burning in or around your vagina, use the applicator or baster to insert the yogurt into your vagina and use the spoon to lather the area around the vagina that is painful or burning. Use a maxi pad or other feminine garment to prevent spillage and leave for at least 12 hours. Most women who do this will do so before bed and leave overnight.

8. (Optional) An alternative to #7 is to use a tampon rolled in yogurt, but you can also apply 5-10 drops of grapefruit seed extract (GSE) to make it more effective.

If the infection hasn't cleared after seven days of this protocol, see a doctor to be tested for gonorrhea, chlamydia, trichomoniasis, and bacterial vaginosis.

Jock Itch Protocol:

Overview: This protocol will help cleanse the candida and other pathogens in the male genital area. The wash afterward will help cleanse and balance the pH, allowing healthy bacteria to grow back.

Supplies: 4 bowls, 3 spoons, manuka honey 15+ UMF, garlic cloves, apple cider vinegar, colloidal silver, 1 quart of plain sugar-free yogurt.

1. Combine 2 tsp manuka honey with two freshly chopped or crushed garlic cloves in a bowl.
2. Mix and warm by suspending the mix in a larger bowl of warm water
3. In a separate bowl, mix 1 cup water, 3 tbsp of apple cider vinegar, 10 drops of tea tree oil and 1 tsp of colloidal silver
4. Spread the honey and garlic paste around the penis, scrotum, and inner thighs.
5. Leave for at least 20 but not more than 30 minutes.
6. Use the water, ACV, and colloidal silver mix to wash off the honey and garlic.
7. Coat the now cleaned areas with a thin layer of yogurt to cool and relieve any burning or itching, restore the skin's pH, and allow the lactic acid bacteria to get to work.

Fun fact: The protocol for jock itch can be used to treat cases of diaper rash in babies and toddlers.

Nail Fungus Protocol:

Overview: This protocol will help cleanse the Candida and other pathogens in and under the nails and nail beds. The wash afterward will help cleanse and balance the pH, allowing healthy bacteria to grow back.

Supplies: Undecylenic acid solution 20-25%, Tea tree oil, soap, colloidal silver

1. Combine 1 tsp of colloidal silver with an application of hand soap, lather and apply to affected nails

2. Wash gently with warm water

3. Apply a coat of undecylenic acid solution to the affected nails and nail beds

4. Apply a coat of tea tree oil to the nail and nail beds

Sinus/Nose Fungus Protocol:

Overview: This protocol will help cleanse the Candida and other pathogens in the nose and sinuses. The saline wash will clear out any dirt and mucus, exposing the yeast and other pathogens, the colloidal silver will kill off and inhibit their growth, and the L sakei probiotics will populate your sinuses and prevent the bad bugs from returning.

Supplies: Neti pot, saline or salt water, colloidal silver spray, lactobacillus sakei powder

1. Add warm saline to the Neti pot and rinse your sinuses thoroughly

2. Spray 1-7 sprays to tolerance of colloidal silver suspension in each nostril, inhaling as you spray

3. Using the provided scoop, scoop out a recommended dose of L sakei, inhaling one dose into each nostril

Oral (mouth and throat) Fungus Protocol:

Overview: This protocol will help cleanse the Candida from your mouth and throat eliminating embarrassing symptoms like halitosis.

Supplies: Tea tree oil and coconut oil, zinc and vitamin C lozenges, toothbrush, floss, antifungal toothpaste (like the Biocidin toothpaste or similar)

1. Brush your teeth thoroughly with antifungal toothpaste

2. Floss in between each tooth to clean out microbes growing between them

3. Take a swig of coconut oil and tea tree oil and swish around in your mouth for 5 minutes making sure to coat all of your teeth and tongue without swallowing the mixture. Spit afterwards.

4. Suck on the vitamin C and zinc lozenges throughout the day to keep the mouth and throat free of pathogens

Incomplete Treatment, Treatment resistance, or other Underlying Conditions:

If you've completed the core plan, and the appropriate specific plans, and still aren't getting better, here are some of the most common reasons why people don't fully recover from Candida:

- They did everything right during Phase 1 – 3 but after they started feeling better they started slipping and Candida was allowed to take hold again
- They needed one or more additional cleansing and detox cycles to clear the yeast overgrowth
- They didn't fully give up drinking alcohol or eating sugar. Even one drink, one soda, one piece of candy in a week is enough to open the door for Candida again.
- The underlying cause of why they are ill is actually due to a virus, bacteria, parasite, injury, toxin, or other issue and either testing wasn't done, or the right tests weren't done.
- They continue to live a high-stress life that impairs their body's ability to stay healthy
- They don't really want to be healthy because if they were healthy they would have to change their lives in a way that is scary, or stressful, and so they sabotage themselves.

Detoxification

The second half of the core protocol is how to detox and support your body and organs while you do it. Candida produces some nasty toxins while it's alive, and even more after it dies, forcing your body to the limit to process and filter them out before they cause damage and an increase in symptoms. Luckily, there are many options and things we can do and take in preparation to make things as easy as possible. The following are some of the most important during phase 1 and 2:

- Sleep – sleep is one of the most fundamental and important processes to staying healthy. It's unfortunate that so many health issues cause us to lose sleep. There are several things we can do to improve and ensure good quality sleep
  - Keep the temperature cool, ideally at 65 degrees
  - Go to sleep and wake up at the same time each day
  - Avoid technology for 2 hours before sleeping
  - Avoid exposure to white or blue light within 2 hours of sleeping
  - Avoid eating within 4 hours of sleeping
  - Engage in relaxing activity before bed
  - Exercise regularly
  - Get exposure to bright light, ideally sunlight, first thing in the morning
  - Limit caffeine intake after noon
  - You can use natural sleep aids like melatonin, GABA, l-theanine, valerian root, and others as needed

- Hydration – aim for a minimum of 80 ounces of water per day, and ideally between 120 and 160 to ensure the clearing of urinary toxins. This can deplete your electrolytes so ensure you are getting enough through diet or supplementation.

- Sweating – Expelling toxins through your skin is one of the primary ways you detox. Exercising until you sweat, relaxing in a sauna or hot bath, or other activities that force your body to sweat are all good ways to eliminate the increased toxins you'll be generating while killing off Candida.

- Bowel movements – If you aren't pooping every day while on this protocol then something is wrong. Your bowels need to be moving to ensure that toxins are not building up in your gut and bile and then recirculating back into your blood and body. During this process it's better to have looser stools than be constipated. If you are on the more constipated side try increasing the amount of fiber you are eating, adding an additional 500mg of magnesium oxide, or 1-5 grams of vitamin C to help move things along.

- Supplements – there are dozens of supplements that can help with detox, but we are going to limit it to a few core types. First, we have botanicals that boost the function of your detox organs, immune system, and some of them even have antifungal properties. These include:
  - Chinese skullcap – helps support the body and restores the microbiome
  - Bacopa monieri – which is a potent antifungal and can aid in with cognition

77

- Gotu Kola – which is an antifungal and can help the body with stress and circulation

Next, we have supplements that specifically support one or more of the organs used in detoxification. These include:

- Milk thistle – protects the liver
- Cranberry – helps cleanse the kidneys
- Astralagus – helps support the kidneys
- N Acetyl Cysteine (NAC) – supports and regenerates the liver

Last, we have some generic detox supplements that help clean up the mess caused by the dying Candida and other pathogens.

- Molybdenum – reduces the buildup of acetaldehyde which is the primary toxin released by many strains of Candida
- Activated charcoal – scavenges your gut for toxins released by the Candida and other microbes
- Bentonite or zeolite clay – often used in combination to scavenge for toxins in a similar way to activated charcoal
- Red clover tea – used up to 4 cups per day, to increase blood flow in the body, allowing the kidneys to process out more toxins
- Epsom salts – a type of magnesium that helps draw toxins out of the body. Not ingested but rather added to a bath or other soak.

Typically, clients will use a combination of these supplements based on their symptoms, and the specific herbs used in the cleansing half of the protocol. Some of these, like activated charcoal, NAC, and molybdenum are more broadly beneficial, so you'll get a greater bang for your buck. None of them are absolutely necessary, but all will improve your symptoms, so if you can afford it, you'll be doing yourself a huge favor by investing in one or more of these.

Now, if your symptoms are really bad, especially within hours or days of starting antifungals or other antimicrobials, you might be having what is called a Jarisch-Herxheimer reaction, otherwise known as a Herx. This is a syndrome where your detox organs are overloaded and can't deal with all of the toxins and cytokines (think inflammation) that is happening and you feel terrible as a result, possibly worse than you've ever felt. For that we've included a plan that is battle tested with many clients and practitioners to quickly get you out of a Herx state and back on track with healing. Keep in mind this isn't magic, but I haven't seen a client who followed these steps who did not start feeling better.

The Plan for Jarisch-Herxheimer Reactions (Herx):

1. Alkalize: Alka seltzer, sodium bicarbonate, buffered Vitamin C, or lemon-lime water (1-2 of each in water) drink during onset
2. Support elimination: glutathione, NAC, milk thistle, ALA, B vitamins, dandelion, charcoal, bentonite, zeolite, cholestyramine, and or enemas
3. Stop cytokines: LDN and antioxidants like ALA, glutathione, resveratrol, curcumin, glucoraphanin and sulforaphane, FSM, or grounding
4. Supplement the minerals depleted by detox: magnesium, zinc, and copper

5. Open up drainage pathways: exercise, extra fluids, sleep, sauna, and supplements like parsley and burbur pinella.

Chapter 5: Phase 3 – Restoring Your Health

"John had battled an autoimmune disease for years, experiencing relentless fatigue and debilitating pain that no treatment seemed to alleviate. After countless doctor visits and failed medications, he stumbled upon the connection between Candida overgrowth and autoimmune conditions. Skeptical but desperate, he overhauled his diet, incorporated anti-Candida herbs, and embraced a holistic approach to healing. Within months, John's symptoms began to fade, and his energy returned. Today, he lives a vibrant life, running marathons, enjoying time with his family, and sharing his story to inspire others. His journey from chronic illness to health has been nothing short of miraculous, proving the profound impact of addressing Candida."

Our goal with this book is to help you in the same way that John had his health restored, with a focus on gut health and regulating immunity. These two core functions within the body help govern and regulate what microbes are allowed and where they can live. If our gut is happy, healthy, and well-supplied with nutrients, it helps support all our other organs and body systems, including the immune system. When the immune system is happy and supported, the pathogens are limited or eliminated, the body has more time and energy to focus on other processes, the distinction between self and other is maintained which reduces or eliminates autoimmunity, and so like we discussed in Chapter 1, the functions of our body are all interconnected, and the dominoes of autoimmunity can be addressed holistically, and you can get better, even when conventional medicine and wisdom might be against you.

Now, we've already talked a great deal about gut health, digestion and the microbiome. There are a few more classes of supplements we need to look at in this phase that aren't appropriate in the earlier phases, but now, after the killing is done, we can repopulate the gut with good bacteria, and improve the condition of the gut to make good bugs more likely to stay. There are two major classes of good bugs that we want to look at: those that compete directly with Candida for real estate in your gut and can therefore crowd it out, and those that produce useful chemicals that our bodies need.

The first group, which includes bacteria like L crispatus, L sakei, and L plantarum, but also fungi like Saccharomyces boulardii, competes with Candida for food and binding sites. This directly reduces Candida levels, and supplementing with these probiotics can prevent the recurrence of Candida infection.

The second group is microbes that produce useful chemicals like neurotransmitters, B vitamins, short-chain fatty acids, and lactic acid. Bacteria that produce neurotransmitters include:

- Serotonin – is produced by Streptococcus, Enterococcus, Escherichia, Lactobacillus, Klebsiella, and Morganella bacteria

- Dopamine – is produced by Lactobacillus, Serratia, Bacillus, Morganella, and Klebsiella bacteria
- Norepinephrine is produced by Lactobacillus, Serratia, Bacillus, Morganella and Klebsiella bacteria
- GABA is produced by strains of Lactobacillus and Bifidobacteria

As you can see it's a collaboration of many bacteria that produce the neurotransmitters needed to keep us functioning and healthy. B vitamins are produced by a collection of Bifidobacterium, Clostridium, Enterococcus, and Bacteroides. Short chain fatty acids like butyrate, propionate, and acetate, are produced by Bacteroides, Firmicutes, and Actinobacteria and finally lactic acid producers are far and away the biggest group, but most of them are covered in the bacterial families already listed. Without these chemicals, we as human beings wouldn't be able to function. When we have high levels of Candida, or an overgrowth, many of these critically important bacteria get crowded out by the fast growing Candida, or starved out as Candida will consume the food they need higher up in the digestive tract and so it won't make it down to areas like the terminal ileum which is close to where most of the B vitamins are made. Part of this recovery process then is to ensure that the right bacteria and microbes are living in your gut and you can do that by supplementing strains, based on need. That needed is typically determined based on symptoms in that if your mood is low, it makes sense to supplement with probiotics that produce B vitamins and neurotransmitters, if gut health is an issue, supplement with microbes that produce short chain fatty acids, and for nearly everyone reading this book and on a Candida protocol, supplementing with lactic acid producing bacteria as that lactic acid will balance the pH of the gut and make it more difficult for Candida to thrive.

In addition to probiotics, we can supplement with prebiotics to improve the quality of our gut health and microbiome. These prebiotics are mostly fibers that provide food for beneficial bacteria, while not being edible for the bad bacteria. Examples of prebiotics include:

- Inulin

- Chicory

- Garlic

- Leeks

- The fiber or pulp from most vegetables

The oxygen level of the gut makes a difference in the type of bacteria that live there as well. The small intestine should be almost entirely anaerobic, that is without oxygen, and the bacteria that live there should be mostly nitrogen breathers. When the gut is disrupted and the microbiome changes, there is often an influx of oxygen breathing and producing bacteria in the small intestine which makes it difficult for the nitrogenous bacteria to live and thrive there creating a cycle of dysbiosis that's hard to fix. Butyrate, one of those short chain fatty acids that we mentioned earlier, can reduce the oxygen in the gut, allowing more of the nitrogenous bacteria back into the small intestine, and potentially fixing the issue until enough SCFA producing bacteria have been cultivated to take over the butyrate production. This butyrate production is also incredibly important to the function of the gut immune system and adequate production of it is a big step in breaking the cycle of autoimmunity present in many patients.

To continue healing the gut there are many nutrients that can accelerate the process. Some of them we talked about in the section on reducing gut inflammation and some will be new. Here's a list of what can help:

- Aloe vera
- Glutamine
- Zinc carnosine
- Marshmallow root
- *Deglycyrrhizinated licorice*
- *Slippery elm*
- *Mucin*
- *Cat's claw*

Once the gut is healed and reseeded with good bacteria it's time to reset the immune system. This part is especially important in those people with autoimmune diseases as some of those autoimmunity dominoes might still be falling, but there are two classes of supplements or medications that can help reset the immune system to allow for better recognition of friend or foe and restore that commensalism both with Candida, but also other microbes that share our body.

The first of these is low-dose naltrexone (LDN), which is a drug used to help addicts withdraw from narcotics. The low dose refers to a much smaller dose than is used for that purpose, as the dosing used for the immune system is between 1 and 4.5

mg per day starting on the lower end and increasing by 1mg per week until you reach a maintenance dose. This therapy has shown tremendous success in improving many autoimmune diseases, including Crohn's disease, one of the autoimmune diseases where a primary subtype is characterized by an autoimmune reaction to Candida.

Oral immunoglobulins like colostrum are the next class of immune-modulating supplements that can help with treatment. These immune cells, extracted from cow colostrum, taste great, almost like a milkshake, and can have very positive effects in regulating the gut and improving the immune system, especially in people with a lot of viral reactivations like EBV. They also have the side benefit of increasing the gut's ability to actively regulate the populations of gut microbes like Candida.

Either alone or in combination, these two have been shown to bring about dramatic improvements in patients who otherwise weren't getting better. They also excel at closing the door on Candida and other gut infections by boosting immune function to the point where it's difficult for pathogens to create the opening that they need to infect, proliferate, and cause symptoms.

Chapter 6: Phase 4 – Staying Healthy for Good

"Years ago, I struggled with debilitating health issues that cast a shadow over every aspect of my life. Daily activities were a challenge. I moved through life in a constant fog, and my future seemed bleak. Tired of the pain and determined to change my fate, I embarked on a journey of healing, adopting a holistic medicine approach to wellness. Through a healing diet, regular exercise, a Candida cleanse, and a focus on mental health, I gradually regained my strength, health, and sanity. Today, I live a life filled with blessings and abundance. I wake up each morning with energy and gratitude, embracing the opportunities each day brings. Surrounded by loving family and friends, I thrive in a state of well-being I once thought impossible."

There's nothing that feels better than being healthy, but it's funny how our mind works and how insidious disease is. It usually doesn't overwhelm you all at once; it creeps in, slowly and quietly, each day is a fraction of a percent worse than the day before, until you wake up sick and diseased and willing to do anything to put an end to it and be healthy again. Remember that feeling, the motivation that brought you here.

To find health and hope amidst the pain, and don't let that feeling go once you are healthy. Keep doing the work, consolidate your gains, keep eating well, keep living well, and push for ever-increasing health, vitality, and abundant energy that's within your reach.

In this final chapter, we will discuss how we can do that—how we can continue this path of health and freedom, prevent the recurrence of Candida, and press onward into the future. This path is broken down into a few simple steps: avoidance, diet, and habits.

Avoidance is the simplest but also the most difficult as you must avoid the things that make Candida infection and recurrence likely. That's following all the dietary restrictions outlined in the diet section, like no sugar, no alcohol, no grains, and for some people, that seems to translate into no fun. It's not that this is an absolute life sentence, but unfortunately, just due to how we work as human beings, each indulgence increases the chance of Candida's recurrence, and each instance of indulgence increases the chance of giving in to more indulgence. Avoiding exposure to Candida directly is also important and can include the avoidance of some pets, and even some people with Candida infections. It's interesting after you've cleared Candida, how quickly and distinctly you recognize the smell of Candida on the breath of another person and how quickly you recoil. It's like we have an innate warning system in our brains that knows how harmful it can be and can tell when people or animals are infected and tries to keep us away, and if we don't, especially if we date or otherwise have a relationship with someone with Candida issues, it becomes a large daily exposure to millions of Candida, and can single-handedly bring back a massive overgrowth. This brings up another important topic that family, close friends, and pets need to also be treated and go through the same protocol that you are to avoid continuous reinfection with Candida. It doesn't have to be adversarial but rather give them a copy of this book so they understand what's going on, and make it a shared collaboration or journey that you go on together towards better health. Shared experience and camaraderie, especially when you are dealing with the pains of sugar cravings and Candida die-off, can be incredibly helpful in keeping you on track when you might otherwise slip.

Diet is the next major factor in staying healthy for good. While you won't need to adhere strictly to healing diets after the protocol is done, many people end up doing so because of how they feel. Healthy eating, once you've done it for long enough and your microbiome changes, feels good. Once you start waking up clear-headed with abundant energy, it's hard to go back to being sluggish and not being awake without a cup or two of coffee. Many of the restrictions, but not foods to avoid, can be lifted, and some foods otherwise not on a diet can be reintroduced, and in many people without restriction. Fruits, especially berries, can largely be eaten without issue. Some grains, especially ancient or whole grains, can be tested and reintroduced. Most of this reintroduction is based on your tolerance in that after you do this protocol and are healthy, your body will be quick to let you know when it doesn't like a food, and you won't feel good after eating it, so pay attention to what your body is telling you. This holds true whether it's whole categories of foods like sweets, grains, or dairy, or less commonly, nuts or types of meat. Frequently though, what your body is picking up on and pitching a fit about are the toxins, antibiotics, and other synthetic and potentially

89

harmful ingredients in the foods. I've seen it time and time again and have experienced it personally. For example, commercially processed foods like coffees from major brands now taste plasticky, but the organic pesticide-free brands taste great. Some meats, whether burgers or hotdogs, start to taste foul, but the organic pasture-raised variants taste great. Now that your body is free of the junk, it doesn't want it back, and that's a good thing. Candida is also no longer exerting the influence that it once did on your taste buds and your taste and food cravings will change. This is normal, go with it, and enjoy the foods you might have avoided before when you were hooked on sugar.

Lastly, let's talk about habits. We've gone over many incredibly important habits like how to improve sleep, how to improve digestion, getting good exercise, relaxing to switch the vagus nerve state, using antifungal mouthwash or oils, fasting, and these should all be continued and made part of your routine. There are even some additional habits that can help various aspects of your health such as:

- Breathing exercises—Tummo or Wim Hof breathing techniques hyper-oxygenate your cells and mobilize your immune system, and box or 4-7-8 breathing is meant to calm you down and switch your vagal state over to rest and digest.

- Electromagnetic therapies like transcranial magnetic stimulation (TCMS) can directly stimulate the nervous system and vagus nerve to calm the body and release anti-inflammatory chemicals.

- Therapy and emotional work – many books and now studies and clinical evidence are backing up the intimate relationship between our mind and body, between our emotional state, traumas, and how the immune and nervous systems function. Exhibiting bad behavior or dwelling on trauma blinds the immune system, allowing pathogens to proliferate, much like religious stories of sin and evil spirits. Regardless of your religious beliefs, though, the scientific evidence is beginning to show this has a very real and physical basis, and dealing with and processing traumas in our lives can dramatically improve our health.

- Meditation improves our ability to handle stress and anxiety, reduces pain, improves focus and clarity, and can help shift the nervous system from fight or flight like the breathing and EM therapies we've been discussing.

- Nature bathing improves markers of mental and physical health and can even reset your circadian rhythm, allowing you to fall asleep more easily and earlier. Another interesting phenomenon is that many of these benefits don't require you to be in nature but can be derived by viewing pictures of nature or visualizing nature during meditation.

- Cold exposure reduces inflammation and is especially good at reducing muscle and joint pain or soreness. It improves mood by triggering a rush of endorphins, boosts the immune system and circulation, and can induce epigenetic changes that can increase resilience and longevity.

Conclusion

Embarking on the journey to detox from Candida and restore your health is not merely a physical endeavor but a comprehensive transformation of your lifestyle. Throughout this book, we've explored the intricate details of how Candida affects our bodies, the science behind its proliferation, and the multifaceted approach necessary to reclaim our health.

Understanding Candida and Health

Candida, a yeast naturally residing in our bodies, can become problematic when its balance is disrupted. The scientific foundation laid out in the early chapters has shown that understanding candida is essential for addressing its overgrowth effectively. Knowledge is power, and by grasping the biological mechanisms at play, we are better equipped to tackle the issue head-on.

How Candida Overgrowth Occurs

We delved into the various factors that can lead to Candida overgrowth, from dietary habits and lifestyle choices to external influences such as antibiotics and stress. Recognizing these triggers empowers us to make informed decisions and avoid behaviors that could contribute to an imbalance.

Reducing Inflammation

Inflammation is a critical piece of the puzzle in managing Candida. By identifying and mitigating sources of inflammation, we create an environment less conducive to candida overgrowth. The anti-inflammatory strategies discussed offer practical ways to soothe and heal the body, paving the way for more profound healing.

Healing Anti-Candida Diet

Diet plays a pivotal role in combating candida. The healing anti-candida diet is not just a temporary fix but a sustainable approach to nourishment that supports overall health. By prioritizing whole foods, reducing sugar intake, and incorporating nutrient-dense options, we foster an internal environment hostile to candida but hospitable to beneficial microbes.

Cleansing Candida with Herbs and Interventions

Herbal remedies and other interventions provide natural and effective ways to cleanse the body of excess Candida. These tools, combined with dietary changes, create a powerful synergy that enhances our body's ability to rebalance itself. The step-by-step protocols outlined offer a clear roadmap for integrating these practices into our daily lives.

Restoring Your Health

Restoration goes beyond merely eliminating Candida overgrowth. It's about rebuilding and fortifying our health holistically. Probiotics, prebiotics, and other supportive measures help re-establish a balanced microbiome, ensuring long-term wellness. By focusing on comprehensive healing, we lay a solid foundation for sustained health.

Staying Healthy and Candida-Free

The journey doesn't end with detox; it continues with maintenance and vigilance. Staying healthy and candida-free requires ongoing commitment to the principles we've explored. Regularly revisiting these strategies, staying informed about new research, and listening to our bodies' needs are crucial for long-term success.

In conclusion, detoxing from Candida and restoring your health is a dynamic and empowering process. It requires dedication, but the rewards—a vibrant, balanced, and thriving body—are well worth the effort. By embracing the scientific principles, dietary guidelines, herbal remedies, and lifestyle changes discussed in this book, you are equipped with the tools to not only overcome Candida but to achieve and maintain optimal health for the rest of your life

Meet Dr. Diana Stafford

Diana Stafford, MD, is a Board-Certified Physician who has been in practice for 10 years. She completed her medical training at the University of Virginia School of Medicine and completed her residency in Washington, DC. Her extensive experience in primary care laid a strong foundation for helping patients and families with a wide variety of medical ailments. During her time in primary care, she encountered numerous patients who presented with chronic symptoms that did not improve with conventional treatments. This frustrating reality prompted Dr. Diana to question the prevailing approach of symptom management through prescriptions. She recognized that while medications could provide temporary relief, they often failed to address the underlying root causes of these conditions. This realization sparked her determination to explore alternative approaches and delve deeper into the intricate web of factors influencing health.

Dr. Diana is now a Functional Medicine Physician and Wellness Coach who works with patients to achieve optimal health. She is also a Mold-Literate Practitioner, certified to treat mold-related illnesses and other health issues related to environmental exposures. Dr. Diana believes that analyzing the root cause of health problems, not just adding another prescription to briefly allay the symptoms, is the true path to health and wellness.

Dr. Diana frequently shares information about functional medicine topics on social media as @thedetoxdoc. When her recent Candida video became the most viewed video on TikTok on the topic of Candida, she knew she had to write a book on the topic to further help the people who, when watching that video, realized that Candida may be causing or contributing to their medical symptoms.

Meet Andrew Stafford

Andrew Stafford brings a uniquely personal perspective to the understanding of functional medicine. He is not a medical professional, but a patient who has navigated the complex world of chronic digestive disorders and autoimmune diseases, having dealt with conditions such as Crohn's Disease, Chronic Fatigue Syndrome (CFS), Postural Orthostatic Tachycardia Syndrome (POTS), Multiple Sclerosis (MS), Sjogren's Syndrome, and Celiac Disease. Due to interventions both in the book and outside the book's scope, he no longer has any diagnosable disease.

Throughout his life, Andrew has been at the crossroads of personal experience and the pursuit of knowledge, seeking to understand these diseases at a depth rarely achieved by those who haven't walked this challenging path. This deep personal understanding, combined with an unwavering commitment to research and self-education, has endowed Andrew with an empathetic and insightful perspective on functional medicine.

"Candida Detox" reflects Andrew's conviction that knowledge is power and can bring health. By sharing his own journey, research, and hard-won wisdom, he aims to equip others with the knowledge to navigate their personal health challenges.

His unique blend of lived experience and deep understanding forms the heart of this book, making it more than just a guide, but a companion for those on a similar journey.

Andrew has had an extensive, successful career in Cybersecurity and with Diana is now working to bring functional health care to the masses.

Andrew and Diana live in Virginia with their three children. They enjoy spending time at the beach, listening to live music, and talking about supplements over dinner.

Contacting Dr. Diana

Reading this eBook is only the beginning. As you go about this collaborative approach to reclaiming or maintaining Candida balance, I encourage you to keep this eBook handy to continue to use in analyzing any symptoms you may experience, with the guidance of your healthcare provider.

I'm here to tailor the recommended interventions to your personal needs and help you optimize your health. To work with me, you can contact me at doctorstafford.com or on social media:

https://www.tiktok.com/@thedetoxdoc

https://www.instagram.com/thedetoxdoc_

https://www.facebook.com/thedetoxdocmd

https://www.youtube.com/@thedetoxdoc

Made in United States
Troutdale, OR
03/14/2025

29762675R00056